Salvation Army Social Campaign, 1890, by William Booth
Cornell University Library Division of Rare & Manuscript Collections

WILLIAM BOOTH
and His
ARMY

VIRGIL ROBINSON

ILLUSTRATIONS BY
JAMES CONVERSE

TEACH Services, Inc.
PUBLISHING
www.TEACHServices.com • (800) 367-1844

Copyright 2018 © TEACH Services, Inc.

ISBN-13: 978-1-4796-0819-5 (Paperback)
Library of Congress Control Number: 2018940542

TEACH Services, Inc.
PUBLISHING
www.TEACHServices.com • (800) 367-1844

CONTENTS

CHAPTER ONE

Born Again

Dense fog, mingled with the smoke from a thousand chimneys, swirled through the streets and around the crowded tenement houses of Nottingham, England.

On a chill November afternoon in 1842, thirteen-year-old William Booth left Dr. Adolph's private school for boys and tramped home. Turning in at one of the better cottages, he walked up the steps, entered the cozy living room, and dropped his pile of books on the dining-room table. Greeting his mother with a kiss, he stepped across the room to the fire. It was good to stretch his hands out toward the flames and feel the numbness in his fingers gradually go away.

"How did school go today?" his mother asked

as she coaxed another mouthful of food into sister Emma's mouth.

"Just fine, Mother," William said with a smile. "Mr. Hogdon said that if I studied hard, I might win a new Bible. He's offering one to the student who makes the most progress in Latin this term."

"Well, that's wonderful." His mother wiped baby Emma's face and then spooned in more food. "Now please fetch us some more coal, William. Your father will be coming any minute, and I'd like to have everything ready for supper."

William picked up the coal scuttle and left the room. In minutes he returned to place the coal beside the fire. Soon Samuel, William's father, entered. He carefully removed his overcoat and hung it in the hall; then he walked silently to his chair near the fire and sat down.

William thought his father seemed strangely preoccupied. Usually he was bubbling over with plans for the family. For years now he had been telling them all that it wouldn't be long before they would be on "easy street." But tonight he said nothing. He merely sat, warming his hands before the fire.

"Come on, everybody," Mother called as she placed a steaming bowl of boiled potatoes on the table. "Supper's waiting."

The three older children hurried to their places, their chairs scraping as they seated themselves. Mrs. Booth tucked baby Emma into

William watched the poor people trade their possessions tor money, and then cross the street to enter the Red Lion Pub.

her crib and then joined her husband for the evening meal. Although Mr. Booth was a nominal member of the Church of England, he said no grace before meals. In fact, William hadn't seen him inside a church since Emma was christened. When Mrs. Booth urged him to go with her and the children, he always said, "I'm too busy making a fortune."

Tonight William was surprised at how silently his father ate his supper. The usual teasing and laughter were gone. Father's eyes didn't twinkle, his smile didn't spread out good-naturedly across his face. Instead, he bent over his plate and shoveled in the food, neither lifting his head nor speaking. William and the other children looked at Mother, but she didn't seem to notice. She smiled and refilled the plates until everyone was full.

When the meal ended, Mother cleared the table and Father went back to his seat by the fire. William's eyes met Mother's, and he whispered, "What's wrong with Father?"

Mother shrugged and smiled. "Probably brooding over something." Then she touseled William's hair. "Don't let it worry you, Son. Just do your studies and maybe you'll win the Bible."

William spread out his books on the table and started preparing his lessons. Mother washed the dishes. Then she put the younger children to bed.

Finally Father spoke. "Mother, come here."

She sat down beside him, and he laid his hand on her arm. Although she was in her mid-thirties, Mrs. Booth's hair was already streaked with gray.

"I have bad news for you all," he said slowly, casting a significant glance at William. William laid down his pen to listen.

"I'm a ruined man. The person I trusted has vanished, and I signed his note. All my plans for getting rich, for rearing my children in a comfortable home, have been destroyed." He sighed as he looked at William. "I'd planned on sending you to a private school to study alongside the sons of gentlemen." He shook his head. "We shall have to leave this pleasant home and find a poorer one. We'll all have to work hard to keep from going cold and hungry."

Picking up the poker he stirred the fire. Mother gazed at him, a questioning look on her face.

"We won't have to move tomorrow," he said, staring at the wildly dancing flames. "We can stay a few weeks, but we must find work immediately."

William closed his book. There was no point in studying tomorrrow's lessons if he couldn't attend school any longer.

"I'm sorry, Son." Father stood up and placed his hand on William's shoulder. "I wanted so much to raise you to be a gentleman. With your keen mind you would have made an excellent lawyer."

"Don't worry, Father," William replied. "It's not your fault. I'll do my share to help keep our home together."

During the following weeks the family experienced great changes. First they moved into one of the tenement houses down near the cotton mill. With hundreds of other workers—men, women, and children—William and Father passed through the mill gates every morning at six, not to return home until after eight in the evening.

The work was hard and the pay was poor, but William felt lucky to have a job. Times were difficult in England in 1842. There was much unemployment. Whole families worked in the mills just to buy food. The only thing that was cheap was liquor. Often the workers' money went to the saloonkeepers. Men, women, and even children drank in an attempt to drown their sorrows. Many saloons, or public houses as they are called in England, hung out signs—DRUNK FOR A PENNY, DEAD DRUNK FOR TWOPENCE—FREE STRAW.

Samuel Booth never returned to being the happy-go-lucky man he had once been. Permanently crushed by the sudden change in the family fortunes, he became gloomy and silent. "I can think of few prospects more tragic than for William and the other children to spend their lives working in a cotton mill," he often sighed.

One Sunday morning, dressed in his best clothes, he left the apartment early. When he returned two hours later, he was in a surprisingly cheerful mood.

"William," he said, "how would you like to be a pawnbroker?"

William looked at the floor. "I think it's a miserable business for a Christian. It means taking from the poor and giving them only a little money in return. Half the time they can't even redeem their treasures."

"Well, it's better than working in a mill all day," Father insisted. "I've arranged with Mr. Eames for you to start a five-year apprenticeship, beginning tomorrow morning. The pay isn't much better than what you earn at the mill, but at least you'll learn a trade. When you're finished, you can set yourself up in business."

"I'll never be a pawnbroker!" replied William emphatically. Then he calmed down. "But I'll do as you say, Father."

The next morning William walked with his father through the narrow streets of Nottingham to Mr. Eames's office. Here the necessary documents were signed, and William was bound to work for five years. His duties began immediately. The pawnbroker gave him his noonday meal. "At least I'm one less mouth for Mother

WILLIAM BOOTH AND HIS ARMY

and Father to feed," William thought.

Samuel Booth grew more and more melancholy, and in 1843 he died, leaving his wife to care for William and his three sisters. To bring in more cash she opened a small shop in one room of her house, selling pins, needles, and other supplies. While she did not go to church herself, she encouraged William and his sisters to go to the nearby Wesleyan chapel.

William had been christened in the Church of England, but he felt more at home in the church that John Wesley had founded. His heart warmed as he listened to the Methodist preacher proclaim the good news of a living Saviour.

Six days a week William worked in the pawnshop. And often he saw things that made him very sad.

"Why do they do it, Mother?" he asked one day. "A man came in this afternoon and laid his wife's wedding ring on the counter. He picked up the five shillings Mr. Eames gave him for it and then headed across the street to the Red Lion. He was still there when I came home. He'll probably return to his family with nothing in his pocket. His children walk barefooted to work every day, even in the snow. Other customers bring in clocks and even chairs. They are crazy for drink. They'll do anything to get it. The other afternoon a man came in, took off his shirt, laid it on the counter, picked up the two shillings Mr. Eames gave him, and then headed for the pub. I think drink is one of the most terrible things in the world!"

"You're right, William. I hope you never become a slave to it."

"I never shall!" William declared. "And if I can persuade anybody to give it up, I will."

Days and weeks passed. William worked at the pawnshop, disliking every minute of it. He watched helplessly as poor people traded their possessions for a few pence, and then went across the street to spend their money on liquor.

Week after week he went to church, listened to the sermons, and tried to fit everything he heard together with what he saw day after day.

His heart often felt heavy—heavy with guilt for his own sins, heavy with hopelessness for the poor who surrounded him. He struggled with his burden, wishing he could change, but not fully believing he could.

One night while walking home through the streets of Nottingham from a meeting in the chapel, William stopped. Suddenly a heavenly light seemed to fill his soul, and he knew that God had converted him. Although there were people walking by, sixteen-year-old William knelt on the cobblestones and sent a prayer of thanksgiving to heaven.

The next few days were busy ones as William made things right with people whom he had cheated. He paid the apple woman for fruit he had stolen from her cart when she wasn't looking. He returned several items he had borrowed.

As the days passed, his entire attitude changed. He was new inside, changed by God.

Saturday night was the busiest night at the pawnshop. Many times it was two in the morning or later before the last customer left, and Mr. Eames could close up. William believed that Sunday was the day on which he should rest and that Sunday began at midnight. Although he knew that his decision might cost him his job, he told Mr. Eames that in the future, he could not work beyond midnight Saturday.

"You'll work until the work's done and I close up," growled Mr. Eames.

"I can't do that, sir. It's against my convictions."

"Since when did you have these strange convictions?" sneered the boss. "You didn't have them last week."

"Since the Lord converted my soul," William replied.

"Well, you can live up to your contract and work until I say you're dismissed. Or you can leave the shop permanently."

The following Saturday night William left the shop at midnight. When he returned Monday morning, Mr. Eames angrily told him to get out. William walked out of the pawnshop to look for work. It was hard on his mother, but she supported his decision to be true to his conscience.

Soon William and his mother heard that Mr. Eames was beginning to realize how much of the work young Will Booth had been carrying. Within a few days Mr. Eames sent for William. "I'm swallowing my pride," he said. "But I acted like a fool when I kicked you out. You've been a good worker, and I'd like to have you back if you'll come."

Mr. Eames promised that Will wouldn't have to work after midnight on Saturdays, so the boy agreed to go back. Mr. Eames showed his confidence in the young apprentice by appointing him manager of the shop, while he left on a month's trip to Holland.

William was always amazed at the manner of his conversion. It had been so sudden, so complete, that it overwhelmed him. "If the Lord did it for me," William thought to himself, "He is willing to do it for others."

Unable to keep the good news to himself, he felt compelled to stop and talk with people on the street, urging them to accept Jesus as their Saviour. A few listened, but most jeered at him.

Then he began holding cottage meetings. With his friend Will Sansom he would walk along the street and invite everyone to follow him to a meeting which would be held in a private home. Before he was eighteeen years old, William had preached his first sermon to a group of poor people.

Most of the shops in Nottingham closed on Sunday, but not the pubs. William's heart twisted in pain as he saw men, women, and children crowd into the saloons. Sometimes he would climb onto a barrel in front of a tavern and talk to the people going in.

"Why do you go in there? Don't you know it's the devil's ground? How many children do you have? Do they have warm clothes and shoes for their feet? Isn't your wife working at home right now, washing your clothes, hoping you will bring some money so she can buy bread? Please don't go in there and waste your money on drink." But very few listened to him.

He roamed the streets and alleys of the slums, urging people to accept Christ and live upright lives. He knew how the unemployed often slept under bridges. Sometimes they would freeze to death, but the authorities seemed unconcerned. They argued that it was an easy way to decrease the surplus population, and thus reduce the number of unemployed.

William wanted to get these men and women into church He believed that there was power in the religion of Jesus to save everyone. One Sunday morning he went to the worst slum area in the city. "Come along with me to church today," he urged. "It will help you. Follow me. I'll take you there." Although many jeered at him, he persuaded twenty-five or thirty to accompany him.

Along the city streets the strange procession went, William in the lead, his ragged followers walking after. When he reached the chapel, the service had already begun.

"Go right in," he whispered, "right up to the front. Take any pew you can find."

In they went, the strangest collection of people that chapel had ever seen. Church members looked on in astonishment, then with rising indignation. "How dare William Booth bring such riffraff into our respectable church?" they whispered among themselves. The smell of unwashed bodies filled the room. Women took out their scented handkerchiefs and pressed them to their noses. Even the minister lost his place in the sermon and took a few minutes finding it again. William didn't seem to notice the upset. He was so happy that he could scarcely keep from shouting Hallelujah!

When the meeting was over and the unwanted guests had departed, a group of deacons surrounded William. "What did you mean," they asked, "by bringing such a bunch of paupers into the church of God?"

William was astonished.

"Isn't the church for sinners?" he asked.

"Of course it is," the deacons said, "but those

17

poor people musn't sit with the respectable church members."

"Where would you have me take them?" William tried to squelch anger.

"Take them to the side door. There's a room off the chapel where they can sit and hear all that the preacher says. Of course they can't see him, but then no one can see them either. But whatever you do, insist that they wash before they come."

"They don't have money for soap," William said sadly. "They hardly have money for bread."

"Then perhaps you'd better take them somewhere else," replied the head deacon.

William walked slowly home.

CHAPTER TWO

Pawnbroker Turned Preacher

Standing on a street corner in Nottingham directly across from a busy tavern one day, William Booth began to sing:

"Alas! and did my Saviour bleed?

And did my Sovereign die?

Would He devote that sacred head

For such a worm as I?"

Windows in nearby houses went up and heads popped out to see who was singing. People on the street stopped to listen. Two or three customers from the tavern came out to see what was going on. When he had a fair crowd gathered, William climbed onto an empty barrel and began to preach, inviting all to come to Jesus and be saved. More people came out of the tavern to watch and listen. William noticed the tavern keeper standing in the doorway, his hands on his hips, an angry look on his face. Then he motioned a few boys to follow him back inside the tavern.

William looked at the faces of the poor people listening to him. Their eyes were dull with worry, their cheeks lined with hunger. His heart went out to them with love. He knew Christ could heal their hurts. As he preached, he prayed silently for the convicting power of Jesus to be with him.

Then he saw the tavern keeper and the boys in the doorway again. The boys had eggs and tomatoes in their hands. The tavern keeper bent over them and said something, then straightened up and pointed at William.

"Jesus loves you," William was saying. "If you'll give yourself to Him, He'll change your life, lift your burdens, and give you peace."

Just then an egg smashed against his forehead. The boys hooted and jeered as the slimy yolk trickled down William's face. "That'll teach you to take away my customers!" the tavern keeper yelled from the doorway, as eggs and tomatoes exploded on William's face and chest.

William wiped his face and neck with his handkerchief and continued his talk. The crowd seemed more sympathetic after that. When he stopped preaching, two women and one boy remained to pray with him.

When William turned nineteen, his apprenticeship to the pawnbroker ended. "I can't afford to pay you regular wages," Mr. Eames told him, "so I suppose you'd better try to find another job, and I'll have to hire another apprentice."

Weeks passed as William hunted for work around Nottingham. But jobs were scarce and he was only one out of hundreds of unemployed. But he continued to attend the meetings in the Wesleyan chapel. And he held street meetings each Sunday afternoon for all who would listen.

One Sunday evening a deacon came to the Booth home and told William that the pastor wanted to talk with him. William went with the deacon, and a few minutes later was sitting in the parsonage study, wondering what the minister wanted from him.

"William, do you think you could preach?" The minister came directly to the point.

"Oh, yes, sir," replied William eagerly. "In fact, I have been preaching for quite a while already."

The minister lifted an eyebrow and asked rather coldly, "Who gave you permission to preach?"

Stunned, William said nothing. He felt that God had called him to preach, and yet the minister's question implied that he should have asked permission from the church authorities.

"I've heard of your work in the city," the minister went on in a more sympathetic tone. "Your zeal is commendable. Would you like to become a full-time minister?"

"I think I'd like it very much," replied William. "But I'm only nineteen, and my health is rather poor."

"In that case you must have a physical examination. I'll arrange with my doctor to give you one."

A few days later at the appointed hour William entered the doctor's office. After a careful examination and talking with William for several minutes, the doctor shook his head.

"I'm sorry," he said, "but I can't recommend you for the ministry. You're too nervous. A man of God must be calm and dignified at all times. You'd better try some other line of work."

William walked out of the doctor's office feeling very discouraged. Hands in pockets, he wandered slowly through the Nottingham streets. What could he do? There seemed to be no work of any kind available. He was eager to help his mother support his younger sisters, but unless he could find a job, that would be impossible. And now, to add to his problems, the doctor had said he could never be a minister.

Feeling more depressed than ever, he scuffed along and finally went home.

For weeks he looked for work without success.

Finally he decided to go to London. Surely he could find work in that great city. His sister Ann lived there with her husband, a prosperous businessman. William was certain they would keep him until he could find work.

On arriving at Ann's house, however, he received a very cold reception, particularly from his brother-in-law. Both Ann and her husband were non-Christians and were quite uninterested in penniless William. All he wanted to talk about was the Bible and their unsaved souls.

When his money was exhausted, William decided to go back into the pawnshop business, even though he disliked it. Walking from one pawnshop to another, he finally found a man willing to employ him.

The man gave him a job and told him he could live in a small apartment over the shop. William decided to keep the job only until he could find something better. Hope of being a preacher for God still glowed within his heart.

During the day William received the possessions of the poor in return for a little money. But in the evenings he held street meetings whenever he could find an audience.

Every night of the week he walked the London streets, searching for hungering souls. Sometimes he would sing hymns until a crowd gathered, and then start preaching. Sometimes he would just stand on a barrel and preach to those passing by.

There was only one problem—the man he worked for closed and locked the door to his house every night at ten o'clock sharp. The house, the pawnshop, and William's apartment were all locked up tight. When he conducted meetings in distant parts of the city, William often had to run all the way home in order to arrive before closing time. On more than one occasion, however, he didn't make it; and there was nothing he could do but curl up on the doorstep and pass an uncomfortable chilly night outdoors.

When the leaders of the Methodist Church in London discovered what William Booth was doing, they were extremely annoyed. They didn't feel that his membership card entitled him to preach. "He hasn't been ordained," they said. "By what right does he go about London preaching the gospel to the poor in the streets?" The fact that he claimed to be a member of the Methodist Church made them all the angrier. "He's only twenty-two years old—" they said "—much too young to be ordained."

At the end of 1851 the church refused to issue William a new membership card. That was a terrible blow. "Without the card I don't see how I can continue preaching," he wrote his mother. His dislike for pawnshop work was stronger than ever. His heart went out to the women he saw coming day after day to raise a little money on their pitiful possessions. He saw more than one weep as she exchanged some item for a few shillings so she could buy food for her children.

One Sunday afternoon, walking along the London docks, he saw a ship being loaded for Australia. "Maybe I could serve the Lord in Australia," he thought. That evening he wrote to the colonial office, "I am prepared to go to Australia or New Zealand as a preacher." Soon the reply came, asking which church would support him and whether he had been ordained. Sadly he gave up the idea of being a missionary preacher to a far-off country.

Then the notion that his mission field was the great city of London itself began crossing his mind. Whenever he thought of going somewhere else, the idea returned.

About this time a serious controversy was raging in the Methodist Church. One group of leaders broke away from the main body and called themselves the New Connection, or the Reformers.

E. H. Rabbits, a wealthy businessman, belonged to the New Connection. Another New Connection member, Catherine Mumford, had heard of William's street preaching, and recommended him to Mr. Rabbits. So in the spring of 1852 Mr. Rabbits came to the pawnshop.

"The time has come, Mr. Booth, for you to give

up your regular work and become a full-time preacher," Mr. Rabbits urged.

"But, Mr. Rabbits, that's out of the question," replied William. "I haven't been ordained. No church would hire me as pastor. I've done some street preaching, and I'll continue to do so as long as there are people willing to listen to the gospel."

"I'm not suggesting that you become the pastor of a church. I feel sure that you have a future in the field of public evangelism. Instead of having evangelistic services in the streets, you can hold them in our chapels."

"But who will support me while I'm doing this type of evangelism? I can't live on air you know."

Mr. Rabbits slapped both hands down on his knees and laughed.

"Of course not, of course not! I'm not exactly a poor man, Mr. Booth, and I'm prepared to supply your full salary for a period of three months. How much do you think you would need to live on?"

William did some fast figuring. He would need money for food, housing, and now and then some clothing.

"I think I could get along on twelve shillings a week."

"Don't be ridiculous!" snorted Mr. Rabbits. "Nobody could live on that pittance unless he starved himself. You'll need at least twenty shillings, and I'll see that you get it."

William pondered the opportunity. His work at the pawnshop was assured, while Mr. Rabbits was offering to employ him for only three months. Yet he loved preaching as much as he disliked running a pawnshop.

"All right, Mr. Rabbits, I accept your offer," he said. "And I firmly believe that God is leading me."

"Very good! Give your present employer notice, and I'll arrange a service for you. Only a few of our leaders have ever heard you preach, and they'll have the final word as to where you begin."

That evening William spoke to the pawnshop owner.

"I expect to accept other employ after the close of the month," he said. "I'm giving you notice now that I cannot work for you longer than one month."

"Why Mr. Booth," replied the startled pawnbroker, "if you had needed more money, why didn't you tell me? How much would you need to satisfy you and persuade you to remain in my service?"

"Mr. Tillman, there isn't enough gold in the Bank of England to keep me from preaching the saving power of our Lord Jesus Christ."

So William moved out of his apartment and found a room for five shillings a week in the home of an elderly lady. At a secondhand furniture store he bought a table, a bed, and a chair.

The night finally came when he presented his sample sermon to the leaders of the New Connection. Many years later William was to declare this the most important day in all his life. For one thing, it was his first day of freedom from the pawnshop, and it also was Good Friday. Second, it was his twenty-third birthday. Finally, in his congregation that night sat a young woman, Miss Catherine Mumford, who never once took her eyes from his face.

As the service proceeded and William launched boldly into his topic, he found it equally impossible to keep his eyes from Catherine's.

Following this trial sermon, which the elders found satisfactory, William insisted on walking Miss Mumford home. It was a long way to her house in Brixton, one of London's better-class suburbs. They arrived about eleven o'clock. William escorted Catherine inside, and there he met her mother.

Mrs. Mumford asked him many questions about his work, and how many times he had seen Catherine.

"Only once before, to my knowledge, Mrs. Mumford," William replied.

"And just why did you wish to see her home this evening?"

"Mrs. Mumford," he said, "to tell the honest

truth, I found myself falling in love with your daughter this evening."

He turned to the astonished girl, "Catherine, I trust you'll forgive this bold statement, but it's the truth."

Catherine blushed. "There is nothing to forgive."

Back in his room that evening William pondered his future. He could not marry Catherine immediately. His present job was guaranteed for only three months. He would have to establish himself and have an assured income before Mr. and Mrs. Mumford could be expected to approve. When he called on Catherine again, he pointed out these facts, and she agreed that they would have to wait.

William's three months of preaching for the Methodist Reformers went by all too fast. Soon he found himself unemployed. What could he do now? Having preached for the New Connection, he knew that the regular Methodist Conference would not willingly employ him.

As the days went by, he had to sell first his chair, then his desk, and finally his bed in order to buy food.

One night as he sat on the floor reading his Bible, he suddenly remembered a poor widow living in the same block, whose daughter was dying of tuberculosis. Leaving his bare room, he called on the woman and handed her his last

29

sixpence [about a dime]. Then he returned to his room, sat on the floor, opened his Bible, and read the fifth chapter of Matthew. Then he read the following chapter. His eyes stopped at verse 33:

"But seek ye first the kingdom of God, and his righteousness; and all these things shall be added unto you." The words cheered him.

"Dear Lord," he prayed, "please start fulfilling this promise to me right away. I don't know what's going to happen to me if You don't."

Then he stretched out on the floor and slept soundly.

CHAPTER THREE

God's Minister

The next morning William asked the Lord to guide him. Then he sat by the window, singing hymns and waiting to see what the Lord would do. About ten o'clock a messenger arrived saying that the leaders of the New Connection wanted to see him. Putting on his one respectable suit, he walked to the conference building where he was shown into the president's office.

"Mr. Booth, there was a meeting of the officers yesterday to discuss your future," began the presiding elder. "The general feeling is that you should not be tied down to one church, but should be given one of our circuits, so you can travel from city to city holding revival meetings in our churches. Does that idea appeal to you?"

"Yes, very much." His heart beat fast at the prospect of such work. "It's been my greatest desire to preach Jesus to those who don't know Him. I'll be glad to preach, as long as the general public can attend, and that must include the poor."

"We're agreed to this and suggest that you begin your work immediately. Here's a list of the towns on your circuit in Lincolnshire. Your salary has been set at five pounds per month."

"Enough for one, but not for two," murmured William to himself as he walked slowly back to his empty room. "I wonder if I should have told them about wanting to marry Catherine."

That same evening at the Mumford home he explained to his fiancée the opportunity he had been offered.

"Wonderful, William!" exclaimed Catherine. "You must accept. That's the kind of work you can do best."

"Unfortunately my salary won't be sufficient for us to get married. We'll have to wait until something turns up that pays better. In the meantime I'll do my best and leave the results with God."

Catherine smiled. "I'll wait. If I don't marry you, I shall never marry."

So William made his plans and started out. The first Sunday he preached in Spaulding to the largest congregation he had yet met. The follow-

Some of the young people even sat on the rafters.

ing Sunday he was in Donnington, where fourteen persons came forward to give their hearts to God. Then he went to Swineshead Bridge, a rather small church, but even there six persons came forward for prayer. Around and around his circuit he went.

William tried to write one letter a week to Catherine. In them he told her of his problems, as well as of the success God was giving him. She wrote to him nearly every day, giving good advice and encouraging him to look continually to God for guidance.

To close his meetings William invited those who had not accepted Jesus as their Saviour to come forward and kneel at the altar. After dismissing the congregation he would step down and talk with these people, counseling them, praying with them, encouraging them. One afternoon an elderly man said to him, "I've come to see if Christ can wash a heart that is hard as rock and black as hell."

"Let's pray about it," William suggested. So the two of them knelt, together with other Christian workers. Never before had William prayed for a soul as he prayed for that man. With tears running down his cheeks, he asked God to make the man aware of His love, His forgiveness, and His salvation. Suddenly the man rose to his feet, lifting his arms.

"I see it all now," he shouted, "Jesus has accepted me and filled my heart with joy. Glory! Hallelujah!"

So it went for a year and a half, week after week and month after month.

Then one day William received a letter from the presiding elder of the Hinds Street Church in London. The letter asked him to take charge of the London circuit. Although this circuit would have fewer members than his Lincolnshire circuit, he would receive more money. Taking a pencil and a piece of paper, he did a little figuring. When he had finished, he clapped his hands together and shouted, "Hurrah! We can do it!"

The next morning two letters were on their way to London. The first was addressed to the leaders of the London circuit, saying he would accept their invitation. The second was to Catherine, telling her that at last they could marry.

As soon as possible he went to London. In the Mumford home in Brixton he and Catherine planned their wedding for June 16, 1885. Their engagement had lasted three years, two months, and six days. Their married life would last them about ten times that long.

The wedding was held in the new Stockwell Chapel with only five persons present, William and Catherine, the minister, Mrs. Mumford, and one of William's sisters.

Knowing how much Catherine loved the sea,

William took her by train to South England, then on a ferry over to the Isle of Wight, where they spent a week. From there they went on to the Channel Islands.

William was well-known as one of the leading evangelists in the British Isles. It was, therefore, natural for him to accept an invitation to hold revival meetings on the Isle of Guernsey. Although still on their honeymoon, Catherine fully approved.

The local church leaders found a hall and told the islanders about the services. Crowds crammed in to hear the young preacher. Every night enthusiasm increased. By half past five in the afternoon the building would be full, with hundreds lining the street seeking admittance. Some of the young people even sat on the rafters. God gave success, and many were converted.

After their honeymoon William prepared to take up the work of his London circuit, but Catherine had other ideas.

"William," she said, "it's time you were ordained. Do you know why I think they hesitate?"

"No, I really don't. God has certainly put the seal of His approval on my work by giving me many souls."

"I think it's because you've had so little schooling. Why don't you see Dr. Cooke and arrange for some theological studies?"

"Catherine, you're my good angel. If study can

make me a better spokesman for God, then I'll study."

William received a six month leave of absence and began to study with the learned Dr. Cooke. Each morning he opened the great writings of the church and tried to memorize the themes and ideas he found there. He studied his Bible, comparing passages in one section with verses and passages in another. Day after day he strove to learn all he could. He even tried Greek, but found it beyond his comprehension.

Even though William studied hard, his heart wasn't in it.

Each afternoon he would take his Bible and walk down into the poorer parts of London and preach to the people. When he came back, his face often glowed with joy. "Ten people decided to become Christians," he would say to Dr. Cooke, or "Twenty people gave their hearts to the Lord."

Dr. Cooke soon realized that William was happiest as a preacher, not a student. He talked with the leaders of the Methodist Conference. "It's evident that God has sent Mr. Booth into the world to conduct revivals, not to study Greek," Dr. Cooke told them. "The man should be free to do that kind of work." The conference agreed, and William was ordained to the gospel ministry.

William felt like John Wesley, who claimed the

world as his parish. In the next fifty years he would preach on every one of the inhabited continents.

Glorious years followed. Invitations poured in calling William to visit churches all over England, Wales, and Scotland. One call was from the "pottery city," Hanley. When he learned that the people had rented the largest building in the city, William shrank back. Great preachers had spoken in that hall, and he was not yet thirty years old. He hesitated, feeling too insignificant to preach in that building, but the people insisted that they needed his message, so he went.

It was on a Sunday evening that he rose to preach to the largest congregation he had ever faced. As he spoke, God gave his words power, and when he invited sinners to come forward and make their surrender, five hundred responded. Tears of joy streamed down his face as he walked among them, shaking their hands, and praying with them.

From Hanley he went to Burslem, then to Mossley, and finally to Newcastle. During a period of four months 1739 people gave their lives to God at his altar calls. England's newspapers were filled with William Booth and his remarkable evangelistic meetings. And William gave all the credit to God.

As the months passed, it became obvious that Catherine was going to have a baby. But she continued to work with William, encouraging him, taking care of the home duties so he could preach, praying with and for him, giving him advice, and helping him in every way she could.

After their first child was born, William and Catherine continued their life of itinerant preaching. Within the first six years of marriage they had four children, but Catherine and William pressed on, referring to themselves and their children as "God's Gypsies."

One afternoon while William was conducting a meeting in a crowded hall, Catherine rose and walked slowly up the aisle toward the pulpit.

"I'd like to say a few words to the people," she said quietly.

William was surprised. "My wife has something she wants to say to you," he said; then he sat down.

Catherine began slowly, speaking in a soft voice. A great hush fell over the congregation as the people leaned forward to hear her words.

When she had finished speaking, William announced, "My wife has been the preacher tonight," and then dismissed the meeting. A few hours later the people crowded back, and Catherine preached to more than a thousand people. For months after that, Catherine preached. William and Catherine encouraged and prayed for each other as they worked together for God.

London, Liverpool, Newcastle, Birmingham, Manchester, Bristol, Cardiff, and even Nottingham, his boyhood hometown, heard William Booth's voice. And everywhere he went, he told the good news of a merciful, powerful Saviour. Young and old, William invited them all to the great feast offered by Jesus. His converts numbered thousands, and the local churches grew because of his preaching.

In his heart, however, William was not completely satisfied. Most of the people who came to his services belonged to the middle class. The poor people usually did not attend. "Miserable riffraff from the slums," the upper classes called the poor. The big well-to-do churches did nothing to persuade them to attend.

During those glorious years William and his methods were strongly criticized by other preachers. At the annual Methodist conferences, when each minister was given his work for the next year, harsh words were often spoken about William.

"He comes along and holds an evangelistic meeting, brings in four hundred converts, and leaves me to shepherd them," grumbled one preacher.

"Yes, and the glory is all his, and it's his name that gets in the papers."

"What makes him any better than the rest of us? Wouldn't we all like to travel around as he does and avoid the cares and problems of a large parish?" asked another.

In this kind of mood his fellow preachers came to the 1857 conference, determined to limit the work of the young evangelist. By an overwhelming vote they decided to take him from the general field and make him pastor of a small district with headquarters in Gateshead.

Although his heart ached, William accepted the assignment. He went to his new district and worked patiently to bring the gospel message to all. Soon the people were crowding a 2000-seat building to hear him. So many accepted salvation that his church became known as the "converting shop."

Day after day William worked and prayed for strength and guidance. More than anything else he wanted to be preaching to the poor in the cities, but he prayed for patience and worked at the task he had been given.

After three years in this limited area, he felt the impatience growing in his heart. He asked the conference for permission to be a full-time evangelist. But most of the other preachers wanted to keep him as pastor of his small churches.

Then Dr. Cooke stood up and suggested a compromise. "Why not let Mr. Booth spend part of his time as a pastor and part of his time as an evangelist?"

The idea was a bitter disappointment to William. Yet he bowed his head, willing to accept the suggestion, for he did not want to fight his brethren.

Suddenly Catherine's strong voice rang out from the gallery, where she had been sitting, watching, and listening.

"NEVER, WILLIAM, NEVER!"

Lifting his head, William looked at her. In his heart he knew she was right. He stood up. "It's impossible for me to accept the compromise," he said. By that one simple statement, he separated himself from the Methodist Church. Stepping into the aisle, he walked toward the door. Behind him the other preachers sat in silence.

William and Catherine walked out into the sunshine. "Well," he sighed, "that's that." Catherine nodded. "I won't get another penny of salary." He thought of their four little children.

Catherine's hand touched his face. "The Lord will be with us. You did what was right."

William took a deep breath. For the first time in three years he felt free—free to preach the gospel, to go to the poor with God's Word.

CHAPTER FOUR

A Wider Parish

William and Catherine had many friends in the conference. Before they could leave the church grounds, several were trying to get them to change their decision.

"Wait, William," one of them urged, "please don't do anything rash. The conference needs you. The people of England need you. Give yourself time to reconsider. What future will you have without the backing of the church?"

"We shall have solid backing," replied Catherine. "Stronger backing than this conference could ever give us."

"Who will be so foolish as to back you?" asked another man skeptically.

"Our Father in heaven," she replied.

William and Catherine returned to their room wondering what their next step should be. They didn't have to wait long. Soon Dr. Cooke was knocking on their door.

"I have come," Dr. Cooke said, "to see if some compromise can't be worked out. To few men has God given greater power to move people's hearts than He has given you, Booth. We need you, and the conference needs you. Please don't let us down."

"Maybe we should reconsider," William said.

"No, William," Catherine said. "You are not to be tied down to small local churches. You have a message for the masses, and you must reach them."

"Please don't make it final," pleaded Dr. Cooke. "Be patient. Give the conference time to study the problem fully."

"We've been patient long enough," Catherine said. "If John Wesley were alive and here, he would approve of our decision. The church authorities tried to stop his work too, you remember."

"I'm afraid you'll live to regret this decision," Dr. Cooke said, shaking his head. "May the Lord's will be done." With that he left.

Word spread rapidly that England's most popular evangelist was free to hold meetings anywhere. From Hayle, down in Cornwall, came an invitation for William to hold meetings for the coal miners. He accepted immediately and with his family went down to the West Country.

The campaign began in a small chapel, but it grew until the largest halls could not hold the crowds who came to hear him. Men, women, and children walked ten and twelve miles to attend the services. The meetings continued for a year and a half. Before William left, seven thousand Cornishmen had been converted, accepted Christ, and joined the church.

Word of the meetings' success spread. "All England is open to you," wrote a fellow evangelist. "Strike while the iron is hot."

But William knew that this was not entirely true. One by one the established churches sent out word that he could not preach in their chapels. This meant that William had to rent halls wherever he went. Since the poor comprised the largest part of his audiences, the collections he took up were often barely sufficient to pay for the halls and take care of the needs of his steadily growing family.

But somehow the farthings and pennies kept coming. While there was never a surplus, the small offerings were enough for most of the family's necessities. William and Catherine spent hours in prayer, thanking God for His care and asking for guidance through the weeks ahead.

For four years "God's Gypsies" continued to

travel and preach. Now and then a wealthy person would donate twenty-five or fifty pounds. But even with these gifts there was never enough for the family to live comfortably. Gradually the Booths fell into debt.

Following their meetings in Exeter, William and Catherine talked over where they should go next.

"I think you should return to London," Catherine said. "You haven't preached there for several years, and there are many lost souls in that city."

"Oh, Catherine, London is too big for me. I wouldn't know how to begin."

"Is it too big for God?"

"Of course not, my dear," William said. Then he smiled at her. "And with God's help we'll go to London."

The family moved into two small rooms in the capital city. William knew scarcely anyone in London, but he and Catherine patiently waited for the Lord to show them what to do first. Soon a Christian worker came and asked them to hold meetings. "The tent's been erected in a graveyard," the worker explained. "It was scheduled for another evangelist, but he got sick."

William accepted the invitation.

The first night he spoke, it rained. The tent leaked, dripping water from the canvas ceiling onto the audience. Tiny rivulets formed on the dirt floor as water flowed under the sides of the tent. But William preached on, sharing the promise of salvation with the people.

As the days passed, more and more people crowded the old tent. The graveyard was in one of the poorest areas of the city, and the people who came to the tent meetings were the most poverty-stricken people in London.

Nonetheless, William preached the news of God's rich love and grace to them. Day after day he fed their hungry souls with the bread of life. Far into the night he prayed with them, kneeling on the dirt floor, smelling the odor of damp canvas, hearing the praises from renewed hearts.

One stifling July afternoon in 1865 William set out to explore London's East End slums. In the sticky heat of midday he walked through the filthy streets, choked with garbage and litter. He had thought he knew what poverty was, but never had he seen anything like this before. Even children lay drunk in the gutters.

Roaring men and women filled the taverns, cursing and swearing, fighting, gambling, and drinking. Rotting garbage filled the streets with a repulsive stench. Tumbledown tenement houses sheltered as many as fifteen people in a single room. He saw despair on the faces of mothers. He saw cruelty stamped on men who kicked and beat their animals. He had never realized that such conditions could exist in a nation calling itself Christian.

The sun went down, and the slum streets filled with darkness. Here and there gas lamps dispersed the gloom. Still William walked on. It was long after dark before he started toward his own apartment. He had thought his apartment was very poor when he and his family moved into it. Now it seemed like a palace compared with what he had seen in the East End.

He ran up the stairs to his apartment, flung open the door, picked Catherine up in his powerful arms, and cried, "Oh, Kate, I've found my destiny!"

He kissed her. Then they sat down together while he told her all that had happened that day. He told of his walk, of the desperate poverty and wickedness he had seen that afternoon.

"Don't you see, Kate? Those are the people I've been looking for. Nobody else cares about them. There are no churches in the East End. Nowhere in the world are there more heathen people than these."

Catherine looked at him and smiled. "Yes, William. That's true, but you don't need to preach to me."

But he wasn't quite finished. "From now on, let's dedicate ourselves to the service of these poor people. God has been good to us. Let's help make our God their God."

Catherine looked around their threadbare apartment. By this time they had six children, ranging from ten years down to fourteen months. William owed more than eighty pounds, and it was a constant struggle to keep enough food on the table.

But Catherine merely smiled. "If that's how you feel, William, we'll stay in London. God has kept us this far, and I know He'll provide for us in the days ahead."

The meetings at the tent in the graveyard continued night after night. On Sundays, so many people came that it was necessary to hold two and sometimes three services.

But not everyone who came to the meetings came to pray. There were scoffers. There were people who waited to break up the meetings. Sometimes they threw things at William. One night a group of boys crept on hands and knees all around the tent, quietly untying every tent rope. When the last one was released, the whole tent collapsed on the audience. Men and women screamed and children cried, as everyone struggled to get out from under the suffocating canvas.

A few nights later a group of young men came in and sat together near the middle of the tent. As William stood in the pulpit, reading a chapter from the Bible, the young men began shouting.

"That's all nonsense!" exclaimed one.

"Rubbish!" said another.

"Bunk, pure bunk!" a third chimed in.

William looked sternly at them. "These words are for you. Listen to them carefully," he said.

"Tommyrot! Tommyrot! Tommyrot!" The boys chanted in unison.

Suddenly from the rear of the tent came a big burly man, striding down the aisle. As he reached the front, he took off his coat, tossed it onto a bench, and rolled up his sleeves, showing tremendous muscles. He stood there, glaring at the troublemakers.

"It's Peter himself," whispered the youths to one another. A hush fell over the audience. Peter sat down where he could watch the young men, but there were no more interruptions that night. During the altar call Peter watched to see that the young men did no damage to the tent. Afterward he waited to speak to William.

"I'm certainly grateful for what you did tonight," William said, holding out his hand.

"That's all right, sir." Peter put on his coat. "I felt like knockin' their heads together and pitchin' 'em out o' the tent, but I wasn't sure you'd approve. So I just looked at 'em, and they quieted down."

"They surely did." William grinned. "Excuse me, but I didn't get your name." William thrust out his hand again.

"Name's Monk, Peter Monk," the man replied,

shaking William's hand. "Been a prizefighter from old Ireland all my life. Everybody in East End knows me, and those toughs know me too. If you don't mind, reverend, I'll come every night just to see that everythin' goes all right."

"Wonderful! Your services will be greatly appreciated," William said. "But what about yourself? Have you accepted the Lord Jesus?"

"No, sir." Peter Monk looked down. "I'll tell you frankly, I'm no Christian. How could I be and still be a prizefighter, always trying to smash in some other man's face?"

"You aren't happy, and you know it as well as I do."

"What makes you say that?" asked the startled Irishman.

"Because you're living for this life only. When it's over, you'll perish like a dog. You're living for the devil, and in the end the devil will get you."

"Who made you a prophet?" Peter asked.

"My heavenly Father." William put his arm around the prizefighter's shoulders. "Kneel with me," he urged. "God wants to make a new man out of you."

They knelt together, and there on their knees in that empty tent, Peter Monk was converted. He arose a new man. Many years later Peter wrote about that experience.

"I got up off my knees, ready to die for that man." For thirty years Peter Monk remained with

Booth—and saved his life on more than one occasion.

Catherine was as eager as William to help the poor of London. She frequently went out in the afternoons to minister to the sick and dying. One day she found a poor woman lying on a pile of rags with tiny newborn twin girls beside her. The woman was so weak and malnourished that she couldn't even hold the babies. Catherine washed the infants in the only thing she could find, a pie dish. The only food in the house was a crust of bread. She wept as she told William about it that night, and he wept with her.

"Something has to be done," she said. "We must find food for these poor people. How can they come to God when their stomachs are empty?"

William wrote an article about his plans for helping the poor and sent it to a nondenominational paper called *The Christian*.

"I intend to found a Christian Revival Association," he wrote, "and would like to invite a hundred men and women who fear God but not the devil to join me in my efforts to bring relief and help to the desperately poor of our city. I also invite those to whom the Lord has entrusted means to offer it willingly to get this work started."

Catherine and William prayed that the Lord would touch hearts and lead people with means to respond to the appeal. They were not disappointed. One morning the postman brought a long envelope bearing the name Samuel Morley in the corner.

"Who can this be?" William wondered. "Can this be the Samuel Morley who sits in parliament?" He tore the envelope and found it was. Morley wanted to know about William's plans. In a return letter, the evangelist outlined some of the things he thought he could do.

A month later William received another letter from Morley asking him to come to his office near the houses of parliament. On the appointed day William met with Morley.

"Your article in *The Christian* greatly interested me," the statesman said. "Tell me more about what you're doing and what you expect to accomplish in the future."

Briefly William outlined his plans for the poor of East London.

"Very good, Mr. Booth." Morley nodded. "Now what are the needs of your family?"

Booth hesitated.

"Come, now," Morley went on. "How many children do you have?"

"Six, sir."

Morley whipped out his checkbook and began to write.

"There you are," he said, handing the check to William. "When that is gone, let me know, and

I'll be glad to help again."

"Thank you, Mr. Morley," William said. The men shook hands and parted.

Once out on the street, William looked at the check. It was for one hundred pounds. "Praise the Lord!" he exclaimed softly. Actually he wanted to shout it so loud that every member of parliament might hear.

"Surely God's mercy endureth forever."

He hurried home to share the good news with Catherine.

CHAPTER FIVE

The Army Is Born

Morley was not the only one who helped. Other men and women willingly gave so that William could care for those living in London slums. Some gave money, others gave of their time, joining forces with William and working beside him.

"It isn't enough to point people to a loving, compassionate Saviour and urge them to accept Him as the One who can change their lives," William said. "These people are hungry and must be fed; they're dirty and must be shown how to clean up." William's enemies laughed at his emphasis on the three S's—soup, soap, and salvation—but there was truth in his words.

William began soup kitchens in various parts

of East London where the poor could come and get hot food. All during the cold winter the soup kitchens dished up bowls of steaming food for the hungry. William could not understand how the British middle and upper classes could be so indifferent to the misery of people in their own city. But it was upon the heads of the saloon keepers that he poured out most of his anger. From one end of London to the other, these gin palaces lured men and women inside, where the poor wasted what little money they had.

Many times William would start a street meeting directly outside one of these saloons, pleading with people not to go in.

"There's something better for you," he would tell them. "In there you'll find the beverage of hell. I can offer you the water of life. Jesus, God's Son, will freely quench your thirst. You don't need money to come to Him."

William's preaching made the saloon keepers angry. Time after time they hired thugs to break up the meetings. The saloon keepers organized flying squads of young men and boys to make all the disturbance possible. Peter Monk did what he could, but there were so many meetings going on at once that he could not protect them all. Often when William was conducting a prayer meeting in a hall, these young boys would toss burning firecrackers through the open windows. Because of that, William kept the windows closed, even during the hot summer days.

At times young men gathered outside the hall and chanted dirty songs at the top of their voices. Sometimes they pounded on the doors. Sometimes they stuffed burning rags into ventilators, filling the meeting houses with smoke and gases. When William appealed to the police for protection the law men smiled and did nothing. Many of them were in the pay of the saloon keepers.

One evening as William returned from a meeting, a group of young men attacked him. Two or three he might have handled, but with more than a dozen he had no chance. Their fists and boots struck him from all directions. He struggled to keep his footing, but soon fell to the sidewalk as the blows continued. Then the men closed in, kicking and punching until William felt consciousness slipping away.

Suddenly he heard a thud, a slap, and a howl of pain. The beating stopped. He lifted his head and saw the young men disappearing around a corner with Peter Monk chasing them. Soon Peter was back beside William tenderly helping him to his feet.

"I hope you don't mind my interfering with your fight, reverend," Peter said as he dusted off William. "But it looked to me as if you were getting the worst of it."

"I'm really grateful, Peter," William said. He

He scratched through the words "Volunteer Army" and over them wrote instead "Salvation Army."

picked up his hat and put it back on his head. "You saved me from a severe beating. But please don't say anything about this. I don't want Catherine to worry."

"Right-o, Mr. Preacher," Peter grinned. "Mum's the word!"

One afternoon William went to the tent in the graveyard to hold his usual meeting. To his dismay he found the tent flat on the ground. The wind had blow it down. He knelt and examined it. Then he stood up, shaking his head.

"It's finished," he said. "The fabric's rotten. Where can we meet now?"

All afternoon he went from building to building, trying to find a place to hold meetings. One landlord after another shook his head. That night William and Catherine spent quite a while on their knees, seeking a solution to their problem. The very next day someone told them about a large dance hall. Immediately they went to look it over.

It was a poor place, and Catherine was dismayed. "William, how could you even think of holding services here? It's too dirty. Aren't we trying to teach the people to be clean?"

"I know, but we can clean it up."

"But there are no chairs. What will the people sit on?"

"There are the chairs we used in the tent—if we only could find a nearby place to store them."

"But they have a big dance here every Saturday night," Catherine continued. "How could you get it ready for a meeting Sunday morning?"

"I think our helpers will clean it up and put in the chairs early Sunday morning."

Later that day William asked his assistants, and they agreed to clean the place and set it up for Sunday meetings. A number of them came with mops and pails of water at four o'clock in the morning, and by nine the room looked fairly respectable. That evening after the last service they had to take all the chairs out again. Fortunately William had found an empty shed nearby where the chairs could be stored.

As the years passed, donations continued to come in. The number of helpers also increased. William's own children grew keenly interested in the work. Bramwell, William's oldest son, had a difficult time with some of the children at school. Stories of what his parents were doing spread among his peers.

"Holy Willie! Holy Willie!" the boys shouted at him. Sometimes they plastered him with mud. Once a gang of bullies banged him against a tree so hard that it took him three months to recover from the concussion. He never complained, but grew up to be his father's right-hand man.

As the years passed, more and more chapels were opened, some in the worst parts of London.

The number of soup kitchens and rescue homes also increased. William often sat up most of the night, going over his accounts and trying to introduce some kind of order into the work. One man who joined in the work was George Railton.

"General," he said to William one day, "this thing is growing so fast that we've got to have some organization. You're wearing yourself out, and we need you too much to let that happen."

William nodded. He realized that the job was growing beyond his endurance. "Very well," he said. "Let's make a beginning. Take this paper and write as I dictate."

Railton took the paper and William began. Bramwell, who had been working nearby, stopped to listen.

"The Christian Mission," began William, "under the superintendency of the Reverend William Booth, is a volunteer army, recruited from among the multitudes who are without God and without hope in the world."

Bramwell Booth sprang to his feet. "I object! Volunteers serve only for the duration of the campaign. A regular soldier belongs to the army all his life. If I'm going to join such an army, it will be as a regular, not as a volunteer."

His father paused and thought a minute. Taking the pen from Railton, he scratched through the words, "Volunteer Army" and over them wrote instead, "Salvation Army."

"That sounds better!" Bramwell said. Railton seemed happy with it. And that was the beginning of an organization that would spread around the world, sharing help and hope with millions.

By this time eighty-eight men and women were working with William. William was given the title General, as commander in chief of the Salvation Army. William liked the title and seemed to grow fonder of it every year of his life. His favorite song became "Onward Christian Soldiers."

Armies have an enemy to fight. General Booth drafted a statement that the Salvation Army was made up of the King of heaven's soldiers and that they had declared war on the devil, sin, and every kind of evil.

"The best kind of warfare is offensive. We must attack," he said. "We'll carry the struggle right into the hearts of the enemy's country!"

Down into the slums the Salvation soldiers went, walking straight into the saloons where they sang and prayed and preached until angry saloon keepers hurled them into the streets.

Out from London went the officers and privates of the new army into cities, towns, and villages all over England. They marched through the streets singing as they went along, inviting people to street meetings, or to services in some chapel that was open to them. Hundreds were converted, and many of these converts joined the Salvation Army as workers.

"What's an army without uniforms?" asked the General. "In the rough and tumble of battle we must be able to pick out friend from foe." So the women in the army designed uniforms.

Before long the Salvation Army developed musical bands. At first instruments were few, and much of the playing was far from musical. With increased practice, however, the musicians became very skillful.

Soon groups of Salvation Army workers, playing instruments, marching with a flag before them, became a common sight in towns and cities all over England. Down the streets they marched with trumpets blowing and the band playing such tunes as *Hold the Fort, Stand Up for Jesus,* or *Pull for the Shore, Sailor.* Interest grew in the hearts of many who saw and heard them. As the band marched, people would fall in behind. The crowd following the musicians grew steadily until they reached some open space or a park. Then the Salvation Army officers would stop and hold a service.

"We must capture the attention of the world," declared Elijah Cadman, one of the leaders. When he entered Newcastle, he had handbills printed, inviting the people to come and listen to the Hallelujah Lassies in the hall. Filled with curiosity, people came to the meeting hall and packed it to the highest galleries.

Everywhere, it seemed, the army was marching against evil. To keep in touch with his officers, Booth made quick trips around the country. He knew that many of his helpers would suffer severely in their war with the devil and his agents. Once when he was introduced to four new recruits, he remarked grimly, yet with a smile, "I sentence you to hard labor for life."

They knew what he meant.

To keep the world informed about army activities, Booth started *The War Cry,* a paper that has ever since been the official magazine of the Salvation Army.

For several years the army met public opposition in many cities. Unlike the preachers of the regular churches, leaders of the Salvation Army were not willing to preach quietly inside buildings. With flags flying and bands playing, they marched down the main street of town, preaching and praying with all they met.

Hundreds, then thousands were converted. As the saloon keepers saw the number of their customers diminishing after every army invasion, they were very angry. They often hired men to break up the marches and meetings—big mean men to whom they gave money and whiskey as a reward for disrupting a salvation meeting.

Scores of Salvation Army members were injured in the clashes. A number spent weeks in hospitals. William and Catherine were saddened by the sufferings of their brave soldiers. Booth wrote a strong letter of protest to Sir William Harcourt, a member of the British cabinet, asking him for protection. Sir William replied that the keeping of the peace was the work of local magistrates and not the business of the home secretary of Her Majesty's government.

Hearing that Elijah Cadman, one of the Salvation Army's chief officers, was planning to march through the city of Sheffield in January 1882, William decided to go and march with his soldiers and share their dangers. When the day came, the procession formed around noon and set out to march to Albert Hall.

Leading the army was a wagon filled with the band. As the men and women played salvation tunes, Lieutenant Davison, the champion wrestler of Northumberland who had recently been converted, followed on a beautiful white horse. William followed in his carriage. Behind him nearly a hundred of the army's rank and file marched.

A thousand men, calling themselves the "Sheffield Blades," lined the streets, waiting the signal to attack. Suddenly their leader let out a terrific yell. Running full tilt, the "Blades" crashed into the procession.

Hurling clods, bricks, and bottles they tipped over the wagon. The men and women in the

65

band sprawled onto the street. The "Blades" kicked and beat them and tried to destroy their precious instruments. A stone hit Davison on the head, nearly knocking him from his horse. A huge club struck the base of his skull. Only the fact that his enemies were trying to pull him off his horse from both sides kept him in the saddle.

General William Booth had never seen anything like this. Standing straight and tall in his carriage, he took in the whole scene. "Stay near my carriage," he called, afraid that some of the Salvation Army women might be carried away by the mob. Then he noticed the police—quite a group of them standing along the sidewalk watching, but doing nothing to protect the marchers.

Somehow Cadman, Booth, and their followers managed to reach Albert Hall. Some soldiers had cuts and bruises that would remind them of this day for weeks to come. A bystander spat on Booth's uniform.

"Let it be," commanded William as a fellow soldier moved to wipe it off. "It's a medal of honor."

Even in the hall their troubles were not over. The mob followed the army in, still yelling and cursing and shoving.

Through it all the Salvation Army did not fight back. It was part of their program to accept ill treatment at the hands of the enemy.

One woman was followed up the stairway into the hall by a taunting ruffian. "Here's a lady who thinks she can work miracles," he jeered. Her patience exhausted, she seized him by the scarf around his neck. "No, I can't work miracles," she exclaimed, "but I can cast out devils!" And she hurled him down the stairs.

Evening came. The mob left the hall, and Booth spoke for a while to his bruised and bleeding army.

"We must expect casualties in this war," he explained. "Never forget, there's a crown of life waiting for every one of you."

"Amen! Praise the Lord! Hallelujah!" Booth heard voices all around him.

Nothing could stop an army like that! Nothing did.

CHAPTER SIX

To Far Countries

One evening as William was passing the children's rooms on his way to the living room, he heard something that made him stop and listen. Then he went on, sat down with a sigh in the straight-backed chair beside a flickering oil lamp, and placed his head in his hands.

"What is it, William?" Catherine asked when she entered the room. He sighed again, but the heavy feeling inside him did not move.

"It's something Emma said a few moments ago. I was going past her bedroom, and I overheard her praying." He shook his head. "I heard only one sentence, but it troubled me. I wish I knew just what she meant."

"What did she say?" Catherine gently asked.

"It was something like this, 'And dear God, please make Father like he used to be.' "

"Are you going to ask her what she meant?" Catherine asked.

"No, I'm afraid I might embarrass her. Could you ask her? She'll tell you."

"All right, William, I'll do it. I think I know what she meant, but I won't say until I've talked with her."

A few nights later, when the eight Booth children had all gone to bed, Catherine said, "I talked with her today. To put it rather bluntly, my dear, the army takes so much of your time; you don't have any left for your family. You used to play with the children and tell them stories. Now, with the hundreds of letters you get every week and all your other work, you just don't have time for your family anymore."

William began pacing the room.

"She's right," he said. "Of course she's right. I hadn't realized it until now. Why, I'm becoming a stranger to my own children. I'll have to change a few things."

The following week he suggested, "Let's have a picnic in Hyde Park next Sunday."

"Wonderful!" Catherine's tired eyes lighted up. "It's been years since we've had a picnic. Will you be preaching to the people?"

"No, this time we'll have just the family to think about and plan for. You and Katie prepare a nice lunch, and I will arrange for a carriage."

The following Sunday morning William drove an open buggy up to the door of his house. The whole family piled in, and off they went to the park. It was a beautiful day, with the fragrance of fresh flowers, and the flashing color of butterflies flitting here and there. William rented a boat, and they went rowing on the lake. They fed the swans. Then they sat on the edge of the lake and ate the lunch Catherine had brought. They laughed and teased each other as they ate.

William watched, delighted in the growing personalities of his children, happy to have a few hours to spend with them. After eating, they followed the gravel paths among the flower beds. Near the end of the park they gazed across a tall hedge and saw Buckingham Palace.

"What building is that?" one of the children asked.

"That's Buckingham Palace where the queen lives," replied William.

"Does she have that big house all to herself?"

"Oh, no. She has many servants."

"Can we go in and see her?" Evangeline asked.

William smiled. "I'm afraid you wouldn't get very far into the palace unless you were invited. Just suppose all the people living in England tried to see the queen. She has to have it quiet so she can do her work."

"Can't we get any closer?" Herbert asked.

"Yes, I'm sure we can."

William and the rest of the family walked to one of the park gates; then along the street they went to the front of the palace. At the palace they stood with hundreds of other people who were waiting to see the changing of the guard. They watched through the iron bars as the bugle played and the soldiers marched. The splendid men tall and straight in their royal guard uniforms made a gorgeous sight.

"Do you think the soldiers in our Salvation Army will ever look like them?" asked Bramwell.

"No, I don't think they should," William said. "We need all the money we can get to help the poor, and so it wouldn't be right for us to spend a lot of money on beautiful uniforms."

The sun was setting as William drove the carriage up in front of his house and deposited his family. Then he drove the horses back to the livery stable. It had been a day to remember.

The six years that followed the founding of the Salvation Army were probably the busiest in William's life, although right up to the age of eighty he continued to work in a manner that would have killed most men. The army continued growing rapidly. Men and women from all walks of life joined in proclaiming the gospel to the poor. Some of them gave up good jobs to enlist in the army. The General established a

71

training school for them in London where he taught them how to win souls. Then he sent them out by fives and tens to the cities of England. Many of them went much farther than to English cities. One group crossed the Atlantic Ocean and began work in the United States. At first many city authorities were suspicious of them. The New York police had heard of the riots in England that started when people opposed the marching army. When they heard that George Railton and his fellow soldiers had arrived in New York to conduct street meetings, the city authorities quickly drew up a law forbidding open gatherings unless they were conducted by a priest or an ordained minister.

Railton did not go to the the city hall and beg permission to hold a meeting in the streets of New York. Instead he issued an ultimatum ordering the City of New York to lift the ban on street meetings within twenty-four hours. The mayor refused, but the story got into the papers, and the nation started talking about the Salvation Army.

In England General Booth heard about the incident and chuckled.

"That was brilliant strategy," he told Bramwell. "It sounds like a real army in action."

In the United States the Salvation Army recruited many new members. Soon bands were playing and soldiers were marching through the streets of many American cities. Men and women were converted at these street meetings. The officers remembered the command of the General: "Go for souls, and go for the worst."

Before long the poor in American cities found out what the poor in England had discovered. When you are hungry and cold and without a shelter, the Salvation Army will help you. Gradually the people of the United States recognized the value of the Army and gave it their support.

Opposition to the Salvation Army was far stronger in the Old World than in the New. In England persecution continued. Louise Locks knelt to pray on an open square in Leicester and was sent to jail for three days. While serving this sentence, she contracted a disease that caused her death only ten days after she left the prison. Annie Bell went to jail for singing *"All the Way to Calvary He Went for Me"* in the market square in York. In Exeter alone in 1884, six hundred Salvationists went to prison. Ballington, another of William and Catherine's sons, was locked up for preaching in the streets.

On the continent things were even worse. In France the Army met bitter contempt. There, the Booth's eldest daughter, Catherine, led out in the street work. Riots ensued and many soldiers were beaten. Some were imprisoned.

Thinking things would be better in Protestant Switzerland, William urged Catherine to go there. She could speak French fluently. She tried to work in Geneva. But the city would have nothing to do with her or her helpers. All street preaching or marching was forbidden. When the Army went to other cities, the authorities did everything in their power to destroy it and its work.

Feeling that the command of Jesus, "Go and preach the gospel," should be obeyed regardless of cost, Catherine addressed an open-air meeting in one of the Swiss towns despite an ordinance forbidding it. As she began speaking, soldiers arrived and stood on the outskirts of the crowd. As soon as she finished speaking, they arrested her and took her to jail. After being confined for twelve days, she was released and told to leave the city and never come back.

In Germany, in Denmark, and in Sweden, things were no better. Booth received hundreds of letters describing the persecution of his followers in those countries. Many of these stories were printed in *The War Cry*, the Salvation Army's official paper. There were times when even William felt nearly discouraged as he heard how his brave soldiers were persecuted, beaten, and even killed. Once he wrote in his diary, "Trying to make men good is indeed a weary, disheartening business. I wonder why God has not given the world up long ago."

Although the news from Europe was not too

encouraging, reports from Australia cheered William. James Barker, the twenty-seven-year-old officer whom Booth sent to Australia, quickly won the confidence of the authorities. At his request he was permitted to talk with the prisoners in their cells in Melbourne. Some remarkable conversions took place. As he watched the prisoners being discharged, he realized that many of them had no homes to go to.

"We must provide for them," Barker told his wife. "They need a home where they can rest and plan for the future. Otherwise they'll slip back into crime." He began arranging for prisoners rest homes to be established in various cities. Often he went out and persuaded businessmen to give the ex-prisoners a chance at a job.

One morning the mail brought William an unforgettable letter. It was from Captain Barker and told about an Irish woman named Poll Cott. Poll had been sent to Australia as a convict sixty years before. During all those years she had led a wicked, violent life.

Poll's fiery temper and great physical strength endangered her fellow citizens, and she was known to the police from one end of Australia to the other. During those sixty years, she had been jailed no less than two hundred and fifty-seven times.

One morning in West Maitland, Poll went into

a store to buy a pair of scissors. She was going to stab a railway clerk she felt had insulted her. Rushing up to the counter to buy the scissors, she met Captain Rundle of the Salvation Army. He recognized her from newspaper pictures. Smiling, he held out his hand, and said, "Good morning, Mother. How about coming home with me for a bit of dinner?"

Poll could scarcely believe her ears. Surprised, she accepted his invitation. She spent several days in the Rundles' home. They asked no questions about her past life, but they treated her like a human being for whom Christ died.

One afternoon as Poll Cott passed the open bedroom door, she looked in. There she saw Mrs. Rundle, kneeling and weeping as she prayed. "Oh, Lord, save her!"

Poll's heart was broken. The grace of Christ touched her. Slipping into the room she knelt beside Mrs. Rundle, and thus another wandering sheep was back in the Saviour's fold. As William read the story, he leaped to his feet and shouted, "Glory! Hallelujah! Praise the Lord!"

The years passed. Frequently William felt it necessary to leave his London office. When he heard that his soldiers were having a difficult time in Newcastle, he took the next train for that troubled spot. His presence and words of cheer strengthened his tired and often battered soldiers. He always seemed to know just what to do to improve the situation. Once he won over a crowd that came to boo him by turning around and booing them.

As William continued to enlarge the Army and its work, opening up more food depots, sending missionaries into other countries, and distributing clothing to the needy, there was a continual demand for more money.

He was a good solicitor, and as people of influence and wealth became aware of what he was doing, they made regular donations. However, one prominent London businessman refused Booth's request for a hundred pounds.

Not to be turned from his purpose, William invited the man to attend just one Salvation Army meeting. As the businessman saw men and women, dirty, uneducated, often ragged, pressing forward and giving their hearts to the Lord, his whole attitude toward the Army changed. The following day he sent the General a check for a thousand pounds.

Still it was many years before the newspapers stopped sneering at the Army and its work. One member of parliament evidently did not approve of these attacks. Whenever he read one, he sent William a check for another hundred pounds. If it was a particularly bitter attack, he sent five hundred.

Lord Northcliffe, the founder of a large chain of newspapers, poured thousands of pounds into the treasury of the Salvation Army. As a young boy he had come forward at one of Booth's meetings and knelt at the altar rail. Once, while traveling across the ocean to the United States, Northcliffe was at the table when a fellow passenger made a disparaging remark about the Salvation Army. Lord Northcliffe stood up.

"Gentlemen," he said, glancing around the table, "I want you to know that all the religion I have I received from the Salvation Army. I cannot bear to hear them made fun of."

In spite of the gifts, however, there were days when Bramwell did not know what to do to meet the bills that poured in on him. As treasurer of the organization, it was his responsibility to settle all army accounts.

One morning William entered the office while his son was going over the accounts.

"Bramwell," he said, feeling deeply troubled, "do you know there are men in London who sleep under the bridges every night, scores of them? Think what that means in winter. Some freeze to death. You must do something about it."

"But Father," Bramwell protested, "what can I do? We don't have enough money to help all the poor."

"Find a warehouse somewhere that can be used for them." William's voice softened. "They must have warm shelter in cold weather. If Jesus were here, would He do less?"

Bramwell had no answer, and his father went on.

"The Lord will provide, my son. He's never let us down yet."

Bramwell nodded.

That very week a place was found and fitted up.

CHAPTER SEVEN

Prayer on the Train

It was a cold, foggy day in February 1888, and Catherine Booth sat on the edge of her bed, facing a major decision. Should she, or should she not, tell William, about the pain in her breast? For three weeks the lump had been hurting her. At first she had ignored it, hoping it would go away. But it hadn't. Instead it had grown worse and worse until she could barely stand the pain. If she told William, she knew he would worry. He might even cancel his trip to Holland. And that was one of the last things she wanted. Even though she was not feeling well, she wanted the army to continue its battle, and William to maintain his place as General. He must never retreat or cease fighting.

Finally she decided to tell Bramwell instead of William. Bramwell took her to the office of Dr. William Paget.

After examining her, the doctor sighed. Catherine searched his grave face.

"Mrs. Booth, I wish I could give you good news," he said, "but there isn't any."

Fear knotted Catherine's throat.

"You have cancer," he said gently, his voice barely above a whisper.

It was all Catherine could do to maintain her composure. She had dreaded cancer ever since it took her mother's life nineteen years earlier.

"What do you recommend?" she asked.

"An operation might be successful in lengthening your life, but I feel your chances are not good."

"If there is no chance, how long will I live?"

"Perhaps a year and a half. Two years at the most."

"Thank you doctor. The Lord knows what's best."

Catherine held her face like cement as she passed through the crowded waiting room. But her composure broke in the carriage. Weeping, she fell on her knees and prayed for God to give her courage.

"Well, my dear," William said as she entered the house, "what did the doctor say?"

Catherine tried to smile, as the tears flooded

81

down her cheeks. "He said I have two years to live."

William groaned and sank into a chair.

"Do you know the first thought that came to me when I heard it?" Catherine went on. William shook his head, too stunned to speak.

"I thought that now I will not be here to nurse you in your last hour."

Booth stood up. "We must make the next two years the best of our lives," he said. "We must give ourselves wholly to each other."

"All our years have been the best years," Catherine replied gently. "How can we make them better?"

"For one thing, I'll cancel my trip to Holland. Someone else can go in my place. We must spend every possible moment together."

Catherine lifted her hand. "No, that will not do. The people are looking for you, and you must go."

"But I can't leave you like this!"

Catherine looked sternly at William. "You are the general, and you must go. It's your duty."

So William set out for Holland. On the way to the station, he urged Bramwell to see if anything could be done to save Catherine. Bramwell consulted two other physicians. One said that an operation was the only possible hope and that it should be performed at once. Catherine hesitated, but in the end she submitted to the knife.

The surgery only left her weaker than before. The pain increased.

When William returned from Holland and saw that nothing was going to help, he took Catherine to a cottage by the sea. From her chair on the veranda she could look out across the wild waters and watch the ships sailing on the bay.

At this time William was busy writing the book *In Darkest England, and the Way Out*. Through its pages he hoped that the people of England would learn exactly how the poor lived and died. Out of his experiences he painted word pictures of the despair, hunger, cold, filth, and ignorance in which the masses lived.

William wanted to do more than simply point out the needs of the poor. He wanted to help people live better lives. He urged that more poor people be sent to the wide, spreading plains of Canada, Australia, and South Africa. He wanted to limit the working hours of factories. He wanted to start farms where the people could grow their own food. Day and night he spent writing. Each morning he would read to Catherine from his manuscript. Her keen mind and constant faith urged him on with his work.

The Booth children were now scattered in many lands. Kathie was still on the continent. Emma was in India with her Salvation Army husband, Captain Tucker. Evangeline, or Eva as she was usually called, carried on the fight in

London. All continued sending good reports on their work to their parents.

Catherine grew steadily worse. Emma came home from India to nurse her, and the other children were constantly on the alert for a call from their father. He would let them know when it was time to tell Mother good-bye.

Salvation Army officers frequently visited the sickroom. Sometimes they would gather around the bed and sing, "Rock of Ages, cleft for me." Sometimes they would pray for her. The pain increased. It was often accompanied with hemorrhaging. But no matter how weak she grew, Catherine continued to encourage William and those around her to carry on the struggle.

One afternoon Catherine threw her arms around William's neck.

"I'll be waiting for you," she murmured and then sank back on her pillow. She lingered all night and died just as the sun rose from behind the hills.

Soon after Catherine died, William's book was published. It became one of the most talked-about books of the century. Never had a clearer picture been given of the needs of the poor. Ten thousand copies were sold the first week, and two hundred thousand the first year. A book review in *The Times* stated that it should be required reading for every member of parliament.

Every penny of profit from the book was used to help the poor. In that book, Booth requested one hundred thousand pounds so that the Army could start factories and farms where the unemployed could work and live in comfort.

Walking down the stairs from the Salvation Army headquarters in London one morning, William was stopped by a man he had never seen before. The stranger shook Booth's hand vigorously.

"General Booth, I believe," he said. "I have just read the review of your book in *The Times*. You are on the right track. Here is something to help you in your good work." He handed William a check for one thousand pounds.

Money flowed in by the tens of thousands of pounds. Within a few weeks, the first hundred thousand had been received, and still money came. The Salvation Army enlarged its services. There were more soup kitchens, there were homes for the homeless, and there were farms where the destitute would work and not beg.

When Cecil Rhodes, the famous builder of the British Empire in Africa came to London, he stayed with his friend, Lord Locke. Rhodes was one of the richest Englishmen of his day, having made millions from his South African diamond and gold mines. He discussed various projects with Lord Locke.

"I have read Booth's book, *In Darkest En-*

William prayed that God would save the soul of Cecil Rhodes.

gland," he said, "and I would very much like to meet the author. I should also like to visit one of the farms he has started. Do you think it could be arranged?"

Although he was not particularly interested in the scheme himself, Lord Locke arranged a visit. He told William that the South African financier wished to see one of the farms. The General, Locke, and Rhodes traveled by train to Newcastle, where a carriage took them to one of the farms.

Rhodes was delighted. He saw the neat cottages where the people lived, the well-kept lawns, the long rows of vegetables. He saw the abundant food on the tables.

"Do you mean to tell me that these men have been drunkards?" Rhodes asked.

"That's right," William said. "Most of them have been. The magistrates had given up all hope for many of them."

"They're certainly looking well and happy here," Rhodes remarked. "It will be a privilege to give you something to help your various projects."

On the way back to London, William explained that the men and women at the farm had been saved through the grace of God. Booth had helped them get away from temptations, but God had done all the rest. After sharing the love of God with them, William reached out and laid his hand on Cecil Rhodes's knee.

"And what about your own soul, Mr. Rhodes?" he asked quietly. "You have it in your power to do great good. How is it with your soul today?"

Lord Locke appeared deeply embarrassed, but Booth paid no attention to him.

"Well, General," Rhodes replied, rather hesitatingly, "I must tell you truly that it isn't quite as good with my soul as it should be."

"Do you pray?" asked Booth.

"Sometimes, but not as often as I should, I know."

"Would you mind if I prayed for you now? Right here in this compartment?"

"I would be most grateful," replied Rhodes.

As Lord Locke gazed out the window, the two men knelt on the floor of that speeding train, and William prayed that God would save the soul of Cecil Rhodes.

"Amen," Rhodes said softly at the end.

As they rose from their knees, Mr. Rhodes took William's hand. "General, I hope you'll continue to pray for me. I can't tell you how much this meant to me."

An hour later the two men parted in London, never to meet again. But four years later, as Rhodes lay dying in his Muizenberg cottage in South Africa, he remembered the General. "He was the only man who ever thought I had a soul," Rhodes said.

To William Booth, every man, woman, and child in the world had a soul to be saved. Once after a meeting in a large English city, Bramwell said, "Cheer up, Father; did you see the hundred persons who came forward to the prayer bench this evening?"

"Oh, yes," William sighed. "But I also saw the hundreds who turned away!"

By the end of the century, the days of hardship were over. By 1900 the Salvation Army had collected more than eighteen million pounds and used it all to comfort and help the poor. The Army was working in more than forty countries. Ten thousand officers and soldiers were marching forward in the name of King Jesus, preaching the good news of the gospel.

Into Booth's London office came reports from all over the world. At times he would be so happy he would shout, "Glory! Hallelujah! Praise the Lord!"

Officers in nearby rooms would smile. In all the world there was only one William Booth.

The General was not satisfied to remain peacefully in London while his soldiers battled for God in the far-off corners of the earth. After Catherine's death he traveled more than ever.

Wherever he went, crowds came out to see and hear him. Never did he close a sermon without urging men and women to come to Jesus, and he never made a call in vain. Once as he neared

89

the end of a sermon, he called out, "Who will lead the way to Jesus? Who will be the first to come to the fountain of life?"

"I will," shouted a twelve-year-old boy, leaping to his feet, and more than two hundred others followed him to the front.

William was very careful of what he ate. Many times in his later years, leading churchmen and businessmen put on elaborate banquets in his honor. On one occasion a German millionaire prepared a luxurious feast to which all of the church people in the city were invited. As Booth looked over the table with its sparkling silver and crystal, he lifted his hand and beckoned to a waiter.

"Just a little bread and milk," he said.

The day came when he rode in state to Oxford University to receive the honorary degree of Doctor of Laws. For a few moments he felt a bit awkward in the cap and gown draped over his shoulders.

"If wearing this will make it easier for me to talk to the learned young people of this university, then I'll wear it gladly," he said.

Booth, even after he turned seventy, never let up from his constant round of work. He usually worked all day, and time after time he worked far into the night.

"Don't you ever tire?" some reporters asked.

The General smiled. "Yes, I'm tired, but I must

go on. As long as there are souls to be saved, I cannot stop. I haven't had a day off in fourteen years. When I get to heaven, the first thing I shall ask for is a six month vacation." The General's eyes misted. "I'll be with my dear wife again."

CHAPTER EIGHT

Worldwide Traveler

The Salvation Army continued branching out into Europe, Asia, Australia, and especially the United States. Letters came into General Booth's office from far-off captains, begging him to come and visit them.

"I'm going to visit our soldiers on the continent," Booth told Bramwell one day. "I feel sure I can leave things here in your capable hands. But if you need me, you can quickly get in touch with me."

"Right you are, General!" Bramwell smiled as he saluted in soldierly style.

"Don't try any of that general stuff with me," William replied, trying to look severe. "It's father and son in this office." A little more gently, he said, "I don't know what I'd do without you and Evangeline. By the way, have you heard from her lately?"

"Yes, she wrote from Philadelphia. They're still having a hard time getting permission to hold street meetings in some of the larger American cities."

William sighed. "Some parts of the States are almost as conservative as England. But if there's a way, Eve will find it."

So William Booth packed his trunk and headed for the continent. Germany was his first stop. While there, Count Moltke, the chief of staff of the German army, entertained him. From there Booth went north to Denmark and Sweden. In Stockholm he was given an audience with the king and queen. The meeting lasted nearly two hours. Before he could leave Sweden for Norway, he got a letter from Bramwell. As he read the letter, he grew more and more unhappy.

Many of the newspapers in England had never been in favor of William or his work. The rich men who supported these papers had no sympathy for the poor, and according to Bramwell's letter, some of them were printing slanderous statements about William. One said he had banked many thousands of pounds in his own name and would soon leave for America where he would live as a rich man. Others described evil deeds that were supposedly done in the homes William had established for orphans and young girls.

As William finished the letter, he realized he had to return immediately to London. Within a few days he was in the capital, driving swiftly to the headquarters of the Salvation Army. At the headquarters he found Bramwell and a number of officers.

"I have copies of the articles here, Father," Bramwell said, tossing a number of newspaper clippings on the table. "There is material here for a number of libel suits."

"We'll have no libel suits," said the General firmly. "The Salvation Army will not take its case to court."

They discussed the situation for hours.

"How are you going to refute these charges and make the newspapers print the truth?" Bramwell finally asked. "The very idea that you have used the Army's money to make yourself rich is ridiculous!"

"I've got a plan," said the General. "It will take a few days, but I think it will work." With that the meeting broke up.

During the following week William visited some of the leading men of London. He asked them if they would form a committee and examine the Salvation Army's financial accounts and then report to the people of England what they found. Some of the men were sympathetic to William's work; others knew nothing about it. Booth was pleased when they agreed to act as an investigating committee.

Several weeks passed while these men examined the Army's accounts. When they made their report, they passed copies of it to the city newspapers. The committee found that General Booth had been honest throughout his career with the Army. He had not taken one penny from the general fund given by the public. Instead, he had poured into the Army's treasury thousands of pounds he had received as royalties from his book. The newspapers printed these facts, and from then on there was no further questioning of William's integrity.

Having taken care of this problem, Booth prepared for another trip. This time he would go to India and Australia. On the day of his departure a number of his loyal followers accompanied him to the waterfront. Their band played on the pier. Booth wore his uniform, complete with military cap. With a tambourine in his hand, he led the music, walking up and down the pier, his coat flapping in the wind.

From the deck on the ship about to sail, a young man, named Rudyard Kipling, looked down on the scene. After the ship sailed, Kipling had several visits with the General.

"Don't you think it hurts your dignity to prance up and down playing a tambourine?" he asked,

95

a faint touch of scorn in his voice.

Booth looked the young man in the eye. "Young fellow," he said, "let's get this straight. If I thought that it would result in the salvation of one more soul, I would not only dance up and down on that pier but I would learn to stand on my head and sing upside down."

Years later Rudyard Kipling wrote about this incident. He admitted that the General's reply had left him speechless. Before the journey was over he had apologized to William for his rude remarks.

William Booth spent several weeks in India, visiting various command posts; then he went on to Australia, one country where the army had been spared mob violence.

Booth was delighted with Australia and the army's progress there. "These folks aren't like any Englishmen I've ever known before," he remarked to the officer in charge of the Australian work.

"Don't let anyone hear you say that!" The officer smiled. "These men aren't Englishmen; they are Australians."

"Glad you told me," Booth said. "I might have made myself very unpopular."

When he rose to speak, he quickly won the hearts of his audience by remarking, "I've been told not to call you Englishmen, because you aren't. I can see that, and anyone who looks at you and your country can see it also. No doubt you can see that I am English. However, if I had only visited Australia in my youth, I rather think I wouldn't be an Englishman today. I'd be an Australian!" The crowd loved him.

On his return to England, Booth found several letters from his daughter, Evangeline, asking him to visit the United States, where she had served as commander for several years. William chose J. Evan Smith as a companion and set sail for America. This was his first visit to the States. The American press regarded Booth as a great man, the living embodiment of a great idea. As his ship slipped into New York Harbor, cannons boomed celebrating his arrival. Evangeline met him at the pier and escorted him to a hotel. For the next few days, he conducted meetings.

He went to Philadelphia and then to Washington. The president invited him to the White House for a visit. The next day he was the guest of the senate and was requested to offer prayer.

"Now, the rule is that the prayer shouldn't last more than three minutes," he was told. "If it runs over that, it positively must stop at six." William didn't stop at the end of three minutes, but he did get his Amen in before the sixth minute passed. The senate voted that his prayer should be printed in the *Congressional Record*.

William went on to speak to large and enthusiastic audiences in many cities. His great burden for souls never left him. Nor could he forget the poor, of whom there were as many in the United States as there were in England.

He was very tired when he reached Chicago. Evangeline took him to his hotel room and persuaded him to lie down.

"Promise me you won't get up until I get back," she urged before leaving him.

"All right, dear," he replied, closing his eyes with a sigh.

When she returned a few minutes later, she was disappointed to find her father walking up and down the room. There were tears in his eyes.

"Why, Father, you promised me you would not get up," she said reproachfully.

"I know it, dear, I know," he said with a wave of his hand, "but I got to thinking about all the poor children and how they suffer in these great cities. I can't rest when I think about them."

At Saint Louis he faced one of his largest crowds. He talked with them about his own life, his days of poverty in Nottingham and London. He told of how he had traveled through many lands, serving his Master. He told of meetings in England, of the riots, the abuse, the insults, and the blows. He mentioned the thousands who had come to Christ in his meetings.

Suddenly drawing himself up to his full height of six-feet-one-inch he thrust out a finger that seemed to point at every person in that audience, and he challenged them with these words:

"That's what I have done with my life. What are you going to do with yours?"

General Booth had become a world figure, honored by kings, princes, and statesmen in many countries. Newspapers eagerly printed whatever he had to write. Across his desk in London passed five thousand letters every week. It was impossible for him to answer them personally, but he saw that each one was acknowledged. Hundreds of them contained offerings to help finance the Salvation Army and its worldwide projects.

One day he received a very special letter. It was from the lord mayor of London, inviting him to attend a special banquet at the Mansion House. At the banquet he would be given the freedom of the city. The letter gave the day and the hour for the banquet and said that a carriage would be sent to bring the General to the hall.

"Never!" exclaimed William. "I'll walk through the city streets. I walked those streets preaching to the poor thirty years ago, and I won't ride through them now."

On the appointed day, Booth, with Bramwell and other officers of the army, set out for Mansion House. He knew every street of the city. The poor people knew him and flocked to doors and windows to cheer as he passed. As they neared the

With William inside, the king's coach stopped at the front entrance of His Majesty's palace.

hall, Bramwell lifted his hand and spoke to his fellow officers.

"Drop back," he said gently. "Let him walk alone." They did.

Suddenly aware of what had happened, Booth swept his cap from his head. The breeze fluttered his fine white hair. More cheers went up from the crowds lining the sidewalks as General Booth acknowledged their salutes on every side. Then he went into the banquet hall.

A few weeks later William visited a large prison. He saw many things that disturbed him. Men were coming out worse than they went in. He wrote for an appointment with Winston Churchill, who was at that time the home secretary in the government.

Booth talked with Churchill for some time, pointing out certain changes that he felt could safely be made in the prison system and that would make it easier for the men to become good citizens after they were discharged. Churchill promised to do what he could. Then, knowing the character of his visitor, the future prime minister, with a twinkle in his eye, asked, "Well, General, do you think I am converted?"

William hardly knew what to say. He refused to be untruthful, and yet he didn't want to offend the politician. "Well, no, I don't think I can say you are converted," he said, "but I do think you are under conviction."

CHAPTER NINE

Taps for a Soldier

William Booth could not conceal his excitement as he broke the royal seals on a letter he had just received. The envelope had been delivered to his front door by an army major. Magnificent in the gleaming Grenadier Guards uniform, the officer saluted smartly as he handed General Booth the letter. William scanned the message hastily.

"Here, Bramwell," he said, holding out the letter with trembling hands. "Does this say what I think it does?"

Bramwell looked at the letter. Then he rose from his chair and shook hands with his father. "Congratulations, Father," he said. The letter was from His Majesty, King Edward, inviting

102

William to Buckingham Palace on June 24 for an interview.

"Well, well!" William said to himself. "Well, well!" He folded the invitation and placed it in a drawer. "Whoever would have expected such an honor? Do you remember, Bramwell, the day we spent in Hyde Park, and how we went up and watched the changing of the guard?"

"Indeed I do, Father. That was one of the most delightful days in my childhood."

"Just think! Prince Edward was living with his mother the queen in Buckingham Palace at that very time."

When June 24 came, a splendid coach drove up in front of William Booth's house. Booth climbed in and was swiftly driven to the palace. The sentry at the gate did not stop the coach. No one asked who the old man was. By this time William Booth was one of the best known figures in England.

The coach stopped at the front entrance. The uniformed footmen stood at attention as one of the king's aides stepped forward and escorted the visitor into the palace. Down the long halls, between portraits of England's kings and queens, walked General Booth and his guide into the golden audience room.

The king soon entered and shook Booth's hand. "I am very happy to meet you," he said. "I've followed your career with interest for many years. You're doing a wonderful work. I have read parts of your book, *In Darkest England*, and I believe you have some of the answers to our problems."

"Thank you. I appreciate Your Majesty's interest in our work very much," Booth replied. "I know that your gracious queen is also our friend, since she has made donations to the Army more than once. We shall always endeavor to make this country a little better for our having lived and worked here."

"I'm sure you will. I can't understand why you met with such persecution when you began. You are working to make my people happier, and the happier people are, the stronger is their government."

The two men talked for more than an hour. Then the king arose and Booth stood up, thinking the interview was over. King Edward led William to a table, placed an autograph album before him, and asked him for a message.

William thought for a few minutes. Then he picked up the pen and wrote: Your Majesty,
Some men's ambition is art;
Some men's ambition is fame;
Some men's ambition is gold;
My ambition is the souls of men.

The years rolled on. When motorcars became more common, Booth purchased one and toured England. From town to town he drove, sometimes arriving plastered with mud thrown up by the wheels, at other times so covered with dust that it was difficult to tell where his coat ended and his face began. Everywhere he held meetings, singing and praying with people and preaching the good news to the poor.

There were a few more trips to the continent. For a number of years Booth visited France, Switzerland, Germany, and the Scandinavian countries every summer. He tried to get permission to enter Imperial Russia, but the Orthodox Church there raised strong objections.

"It's a church," protested the archbishop. "See, they have the word 'Salvation' in their title."

"It's an army," objected the war ministry. "They call themselves the Salvation Army." So for many years the Salvation Army could not get a single soldier into Russia.

"Come to America again," wrote Evangeline. That was one request William could not turn down. Every year he crossed the Atlantic to visit the people of the United States and Canada. But each year his step was a little slower, his sight a little dimmer. Every year his friends wondered whether he would return.

His last visit came in 1907 when he was seventy-eight years old. The strong commanding voice was gone, but the old fire remained in the General's eye. He found it impossible to complete the tour that year and returned to New

105

York to take the steamer home. Two thousand five hundred people gathered on the steps of city hall to hear him preach his farewell sermon. Two megaphones were necessary to relay his message.

"Here once more I stand before you, but I don't know whether I'll ever see you again," he said. "I suppose I'll have to let the doctors decide that question. But if I don't get to see you again here, then I'll be sure to see you in some other place." Many in the crowd wept as Booth pointed toward the sky.

Down the streets of New York City they marched until they came to the pier where his ship lay. As the massed Salvation Army bands softly played "God Be With You Till We Meet Again," William Booth walked up the gangplank, waving a final farewell to the city of New York and the people of the New World.

In 1910, William was eighty-one years old. On a trip through England he realized that his eyesight was suddenly failing. He was rushed to a hospital, and several doctors examined him. The surgeons were unanimous. One eye had to be removed. William did not hesitate. He felt that there was much the Lord wanted him to do, and the sooner he had the operation, the sooner he could get on with his preaching. After the surgery, William lay for days with eyes bandaged, not knowing whether he would ever see

again. One morning a strong hand gripped his.

"Who is it?" Booth asked.

"I'm Kitching, sir, Captain Kitching. A message arrived for you yesterday. I'd like to read it to you."

"Who's it from?" asked Booth.

"Her Majesty, Queen Alexandria."

Kitching read the message. "Have felt so much for you, and hope the operation was successful. I trust you are getting on toward complete recovery, and that the sight you need so much will be restored."

"Amen," murmured Booth. "God bless her. Please send her my thanks."

The other eye proved better after the bandages were removed, and Booth returned to his program of hard work. In 1911 he made another whirlwind tour of England before returning to London for the winter. From all parts of the world people dropped in to chat with him.

The improvement in the remaining eye was only temporary; and William again consulted the surgeons. Carefully one of the doctors explained the kind of cataract from which Booth suffered.

"What do you propose to do?" William asked.

"I think we should operate."

"Will I see clearly again?"

"I hope so, although of course we can't promise."

"Very well, doctor, I'll place myself in your hands. But first I must meet my appointment on Sunday night in Albert Hall. Then I'll be ready."

Ten thousand people crowded into the hall to hear General Booth. Frankly he told them of his coming operation.

"I'm going into dry dock for repairs," he explained. "I'll not be around for a while, but remember, it's only temporary."

Once again Booth appealed to the people of London to reach out and help the poor. In closing his talk that night, he summed up his philosophy: "While women weep as they do now, I'll fight. While little children go hungry as they do now, I'll fight. While men go to prison, in and out, in and out, as they do now, I'll fight—I'll fight to the very end."

The operation was not successful, and Booth's sight was gone forever. The surgeon could not bring himself to tell the old man, so he asked Bramwell to do it. Entering the darkened room, Bramwell took his father's rough hand.

"Father, I have bad news for you," he whispered. "The doctors were unable to save your sight."

"Do you mean that I am blind?" The old man's voice trembled.

"Yes. I'm afraid so."

"That means I'll never see your face again."

"Not in this world."

"The will of the Lord be done," murmured Booth. "I tried to serve God with my eyes when I had them, now I'll try to serve Him without them."

Although confined to his bed, William refused to quit working. Hour after hour he dictated letters to his army captains in far-off Australia, Africa, Europe, and North America. But while thinking of those far-away lands, he never forgot his own London poor.

One morning the servant brought in some toast and poached eggs for Booth's breakfast.

"What do we have today?" he asked as she set down his tray.

"Poached eggs, sir."

He tried to push them aside. "How can I eat poached eggs when children are starving and women can't get milk to feed their babies?"

Gradually William's strength failed. August came, 1912, and the General was eighty-three years old. The doctor told Bramwell that his father might slip away at any time. Bramwell, whom William chose to succeed him as general, spent every spare moment with his father.

On the last afternoon of Booth's life, a tremendous thunderstorm rolled and roared through London, rattling windows and uprooting trees. Thunderstorms are not common in England. A storm like that was very rare.

"It seems as if heaven is bringing out her

109

heavy artillery to mark the passing of the General," Bramwell remarked.

Booth could not speak above a whisper. Bramwell bent low to catch every word.

"Bramwell, I want you to make me a promise. No, two promises."

"Yes, Father."

"It's the homeless, Bramwell, especially the homeless women and children. Promise me you'll never forget them and will do everything you can for them."

"I promise."

"Then there is that great country, China. We haven't a soldier there yet. Promise me that you'll enter that great country."

"Father, I promise to do my best."

The tired General dropped back onto his pillow. Outside the sun shone through after the storm. Children shouted as they played in water still flowing in the gutters.

Lamps were brought into the room as Bramwell and his staff officers stood around William's bed. Suddenly the General aroused himself, reached out his hand, and clasped Bramwell's. He was trying to say something, but it was not easy.

"Bramwell"—his voice faltered—"the promises—the promises—the promises of God are sure, if we only believe."

His hand fell lifeless on the bed. It was a little

after ten o'clock on the night of August 22, 1912.

The next morning people on the street saw this announcement in the window: *The General Has Laid Down His Sword.*

The news spread in a flash. Newspapers in hundreds of cities wrote about the wonderful man who had never carried a gun, but who had won every battle.

Flags throughout London dipped to half-mast. William's body lay in Clapton's Congress Hall while one hundred and fifty thousand people filed past the casket. Then it was taken to Olympic Exhibition Hall for the funeral.

Salvation Army officers from all over England were there. Evangeline arrived from New York. Kneeling beside the casket those army officers pledged their lives and all they had to carry on the work Booth had started and developed. Then the doors were thrown open, and in trooped the people of London, rich and poor, high and low.

Among the thousands of mourners who crowded into the hall was one plainly dressed lady in black who took a seat next to the aisle near the rear. In her hand she clutched three faded carnations. As the pallbearers, carrying the casket to the front passed by, she reached out and laid her flowers on the glass lid of the coffin.

The woman sitting next to her asked, "Were you a personal friend of the General's?"

"Oh, no, madam," she replied. "But I love him.

You see, I was a poor girl, lost in sin, when the Salvation Army found and saved me. I attended a meeting conducted by General Booth many years later, and I told him what his organization had done for me. You can never imagine what he said to me."

The woman shook her head.

"He said, 'My girl, when you get to heaven, you'll have a place of honor, because Mary Magdalene will give you one of the best places!' Don't you think that was beautiful?"

"It certainly was," the older woman agreed.

"Oh, he was wonderful," the woman sobbed. "He cared for the likes of us."

When the service ended, the procession left the hall. Directly behind the hearse walked the massed bands, playing the funeral march. Then followed ten thousand Salvation Army soldiers in full uniform.

To William Booth and others like him, surely Jesus will say, "Come, ye blessed of my Father, inherit the kingdom."

TEACH Services, Inc.
P U B L I S H I N G

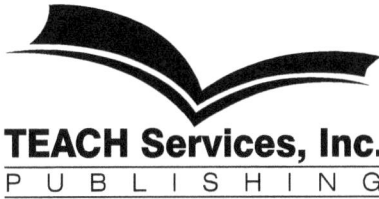

We invite you to view the complete
selection of titles we publish at:
www.TEACHServices.com

We encourage you to write us
with your thoughts about this,
or any other book we publish at:
info@TEACHServices.com

TEACH Services' titles may be purchased in
bulk quantities for educational, fund-raising,
business, or promotional use.
bulksales@TEACHServices.com

Finally, if you are interested in seeing
your own book in print, please contact us at:
publishing@TEACHServices.com
We are happy to review your manuscript at no charge.